In The
Murmuring Trees

In The
Murmuring Trees

*To John Owins
a wonderful friend,
Robert Tirrell Leonard Jr.*

R. TIRRELL LEONARD JR.

To order additional copies of this book, contact:
Xlibris Corporation
1-888-795-4274
www.Xlibris.com
Orders@Xlibris.com
115867

Contents

A Circle Of Friends

I rest my weary bones
Upon the banks
Of grass-grown rivers
Concord, Asabeth and Sudbury,
And sense a ruddy cherub with fizz
Like the face of autumn.

Up where the Old North Bridge stands
Stretching over the lazy Concord,
I sense his laughter still
On a sweet breeze.

The cool crisp air so chills me
As I walk across the while,
Up near that sleepy hollow
Where Sandborn, Thoreau, Channing,
Emerson, the Alcott's and Hawthorne lay
Dreaming like a circle of friends.

Simply close your eyes
You can see them all still,
Walking sticks in hand
Talking as they saunter together
Laughter floating through the branches,
On the early morning tide
Of autumn.

A Post In Furies Winds

I know I differ from the normal view
If feeling better means to be silent,
To let your rage wash over me and vent
For being friends, I shall leave the rage to brew
I know the darker storms are not my fault;
Yet sorrow lives to breathe its spell, to be.
I am the post, which winds blow past and see
As yelling causes rage to slow and halt,
I care to take this rage and turn aside
And see the beauty still, a rose inside.
For you my dear, are ever still my friend
I shall await the talks that time will mend.
I do not take it personal, this rage
I only see my friend with love, engage.

The Curse

Reflecting now upon this scene, I grin
And dream about a day so fear will rasp,
The voice to chill all blood inside and grasp
A voyage deep inside my soul, chagrin;

You see the dark that paints my spirits sin
A door old with the rusty rotten hasp,
Behold a rose that blooms in dark, will gasp
For whom has cursed my days and holds my skin?

I am he, who was left to fail, tailspin.
The image flight, a planes tail wings, a gasp
To fall and fall, as the sun spins, unclasp
A broken will, my self and minds oilskin.

Her whisper blows the winds in prayer "wait!"
Why does this curse, need to be my lone fate?

The Ghosts of Night

I felt the breeze blowing softly, softly
As the wild strawberry moon was rising,
And beneath Towanda darkly, darkly
I felt the breeze blowing softly, softly
On Rag Rock I see his ghost awfully
His preternatural gaze is sizing,
I felt the breeze blowing softly, softly
As the wild strawberry moon was rising;
As old ghosts are dancing wildly, wildly
I felt the breeze blowing softly, softly
A chill of drums echo starkly, starkly
A sad Indian Chief watches prizing,
I felt the breeze blowing softly, softly
As the wild strawberry moon was rising.

Passing the Metal Herds

I'm seeing more the world that I ride past
I pedal faster, feeling wild wind flow
My mind is watching cars, as they get close,
Yet nature has a beauty that's pure joy.
On my bike, I feel again like the boy
My spirit soaring like wild windy coasts,
The landscapes seems like painted life aglow.
As long my heart alone has sojourned fast,
My view of darker shades is dimly cast.
My muscles sore, become more fit, although
I find myself a stranger and a ghost
Yet as my form is fitter, I enjoy
   A glass of tea on my porch to watch the birds
   As cars I pedal past, so seem like herds.

R. Tirrell Leonard Jr.

A Hero's Death

Beneath the moon a hero sleeps in dreams
Medea dances in his mind so soft,
As dampen sands and ocean tides, like screams
The rotting Argo rests above, he coughed.

So Hera sent for Morpheus to sew
A vision of Medea dancing still,
As worms ate wood within the hull aglow
And Jason slept in dreams of her to thrill.

The winds came up and frothed the darker tides
And still he slept beneath the Argo's stern
The rotting wormy wood soon fell in strides,
And Tartarus will welcome home the spurn.

No one will weep the hero's death today,
He spent his love as fools would spend away.

A Magical Country Dance

I took a walk in the darker woods by lake Innatou
And saw the feint lights beneath the veil of moonlight,
As ghosts of Indians were pale and wove through wooded glens
I saw the fairies and fey dance by magical starlight.
A wan girl as fair as fair could be, came for me so blue
Her hair a silk and red as fire, her heart contends
As beauty strove to cast her light and dazzle all of sight
She was the moon and pure of heart, she danced and drew,
My heart away, where her spells are woven kisses of dew.
I was lost inside her kisses, loves laces were sewn tight
Her eyes so blue and full of magic, drew my soul in trends
So now I love the moon and all her light my heart will cleanse.
As fairies dancing, sprites watch on, we danced the moon and I
Her spells were woven through my soul, as love would let me fly.

R. Tirrell Leonard Jr.

My Froggy Squawk

Oh, what a mess I am! As first I fell
And while going boom, I hurt my knee
Its not a far off stretch for some degree,
My accidents often seem to excel.
You see the mess I am? I seem to dwell
On minor spills now and I can't foresee,
As now my voice is gone, an absentee
It checked out yesterday, so very well.
I croak so like a frog, it burns to talk
My voice has left me here, a bloody mess
How can I listen to a poem out loud?
Its like a lightning storm, so dark a cloud
You still can't imagine my pure distress!
It's too funny, just hear my froggy squawk.

Phantom Soldier

Oh gentle spirit! Enchanter of this area
Since slain upon this battle road,
As the fog gathered that April morning
So near to Captain Smith's home.

I feel your presence still.

In your bright crimsoned coat
The bayonets shimmered like wheat or rye,
Waving in a gentle breeze, a handsome sight!
Wrapped in Brittan's majestic cloak.

Wounded mortally that day.

Here your bones still lay
Not far from this marker stone,
As memory has consumed your name
Your bones, here remain.

Oh gentle spirit, enchanting rouge,
I feel the depths of your plight,
Your sadness full and near
Unsure, even after three hundred years,
As to how you've come to be here still.

A lasting victim to this uprising,
At last we bid you farewell.
May the father keep you close,
In the hallowed halls, of heaven's gate.

Oh gentle spirit, my poor young lad,
Enchanting this road, since that April day.
Slain upon a hasty retreat
So near the home of Captain Smith,
At this bend, your presence remains.

Wrapped inside the King's red cloak,
Phantom soldier, with your gleaming bayonet,
Your blond hair lay upon this sod,
As you lay dying, a minuteman closed
Your sky blue eyes.

Not far from this marker stone
Upon this battle road, your bones still lay.
My young spirit, I mean you no offense!
Even though history has forgotten your name,
Your bones, eternal remain.

In Falling Snow

Remember snow falling soft as silk,
Through the forest glens in silent sweeps.
As oaks and elms, frosted white as milk
Remember snowfall keeps.

Beneath the maples, firs and elms seeps
A song of winter nights, which warms ilk
In cascades of snow to wreath in heaps.

Tender beauty seen by moonlight silk,
In winter symphonies, cello sweeps
Sings in somber flows of devil's milk
Remember snowfall keeps.

In Another Wasteland

In the vast expanse of wasted lands
No one mountain is perfect,
No place is paradise
Eden lay in ashes on some phantom road.

As the sun sets in the west
Like a fiery distant star,
I dream of you.

For here within, I find a desolate place
Barren, and burned, though I smile
With you snug by my side
We are free.

Soaring high through clouds
We feel like the hawks and eagles,
Observing a harsh truth
"We are but pilgrims on a wasted road."

There will be no angle to give us Eden's key
No life is left inside the soil,
These days that stretch out before us
Are damned, as even the rats will starve.

The Chill

In through my bones I feel it creeping cold
My touch, I sense it seeping, fogging breath
Yet words will change not this horrible fate.

The shivers start, as chills set in ice-cold
In chattering my teeth and quaking death
The shakes are but a start, as dreams will sate.

The numbness seeps inside my bones and wills
In through my feet and creeping past my spine,
I feel in fears tendrils, a dying man.

The bags of dead and grim of winter fills
My eyes are lead, my thoughts adrift on wine
I dream afar of warmth of summers span.

A warmer sky so blue and sounds of seas
As palm trees sway of gulls and old Aries.

Release

As from moments, I stepped in through the light
The darkness swarmed around me here tonight,
So scratching, biting down my soul, I yearn.

In fusions light I grasped a demons wings
The furies winds influence, holds me still
As bleeding tatters rends my life and soul
A girl had shattered me, a woman cold.

A hallowed ground now holds my thoughts of storms
It said of darkness, "Boy, it comes for you."
It comes so soon, as sweetness comes for her.
I feel its stare at night, a vibrant dark
So soon I shall feel weights of dark release
And then the sun will rise, on the morrow
And then the sun will rise, on the morrow.

The Ocean

The songs of sea, will call out to our bones
As fresher waves will roll in gentle purrs,
Our sails will tack, the leeward wind infers
To dream across the tides and seek unknowns.
We don't worry about dark clouds or sky groans
As forces work beyond our sight defers,
I search for rainbows, in the grey demurs
We ride the winds and sea swells high cyclones.
Yet ripples flow on beaches lapping foam
And topple castles made of sand and dirt,
Or stand on stones to watch the sea and roam
As gulls fly near to find a friend and flirt.
      On beaches white, we dream a little dream
      And walk the shore in symphonies supreme.

R. Tirrell Leonard Jr.

For the Time Being

I haven't actually given up
I've just set it all aside
For another day

If there were some other way,
I'd be glad to hear it
It would be nice

I just need to move
I can't sit idle
Not for a single day
For those dim memories
Would drown me

I've embraced that tower
Dark and moldering
It lay still on that miserable road
Tendrils so bleak
I walked away to the horizon

I simply see,
No other way

A Girl Of Dreaming

Here I saw a girl of dreaming
Where fair but vibrant skies,
Have sewn rare gloss stones, so gleaming
Where romance underlies
Hearts and souls shall sing so brightly
For I hear a song so slightly
Hearts and souls shall,
Hearts and souls shall,
Call on dreams and beckon nightly.

Here I saw a girl of dreaming
Faith so sun on water,
Fair as flowers, fair and streaming
She, the moon's own daughter
Eyes so blue as deep and feeling
Rays of sun so warms appealing
Eyes so blue as,
Eyes so blue as,
Jewels, fair sapphires so healing.

Here I saw a girl of dreaming
While she watched the blue sea,
Heart of hers, so blue and teaming
Moves my soul on allee,
Darkly beckons nights to come by
For we walk and sip the sweet chai
Darkly beckons nights to,
Darkly beckons nights to,
Feel alive, as feelings imply.

A Cloud

A cloudy mind
So falls a shroud
And left behind
A cloud.

I was allowed
A slow unwind
As darkness vowed.

So redesigned
And disavowed
I left unsigned
A cloud.

Fate

A fate so falls before my eyes
The weight so presses on my flesh
It seems I can't escape demise
A fate so falls.

Token, is word to what winged thresh?
As whispers run the world replies
The cards fell here, in darker mesh!

Who comes, yet who goes here denies
The implications of the flesh?
My dream, what dreams have been decries
A fate so falls.

Mists

As mists entwined, my world will change
And spider webs will crowd my mind
I wish across a distant range
As mists entwined.

The dark so calls on waters blind
and leaves a madness reeling strange
As through the fog a light defined.

I fell on craggy rocks, estrange
and saw the fogs of dark maligned
I dream of you, a lone exchange
As mists entwined.

Before the Frost

I stare out where the evening grows
a dream enfolds the blue,
and here enchants my soul in flows
as ribbons sewn in you.
The moon above me guides the way
as feelings steal my soul astray
the moon above,
the moon above,
out where the river flows away.

I stare out where the evening grows
and feel the breath of night,
as cool and crisp before the snows
my thoughts of you ignite.
A fire burns inside the stove
remember warmth and scents of clove?
A fire burns,
a fire burns,
as fabric streaming dreams we wove.

I stare out where the evening grows
and hear the birds of song,
a sparrow sings of what he knows
yet listens for the throng.
A mood becomes one's sole retreat
and leaves one's dreaming quite offbeat
a mood becomes,
a mood becomes,
enchanted echoes to repeat.

Anesidora

The Gods created her of earth and clay
And each so took a turn to add to her,
As Zeus had given men a gifted curse
She would release evils from jars away,
Unleashing curses killed the prayers that were;
Alone inside the jars lay hopes lone purse.

So burns the world of man in stolen fire,
As she will send up gifts of fear so dire.

A darkly brooding God saw man decay
And prayers of mercy floated up in cries,
Pandora did not see her own gateway.
Yet Zeus, so washes sin from her demise
Inside she held no ill will for man's day,
In her, this world of men will soon despise.

Insomnia

The crickets are singing
And I can't sleep a wink,
Tomorrow is bringing
The crickets are singing,
A droning and ringing,
And sleep so near the brink;
The crickets are singing
And I can't sleep a wink.

Last Night

I lit a lantern last night
to relax out on my porch,
vanilla incense took flight
I lit a lantern last night.
Smoking Cigars by starlight
they seemed to dance like a torch
I lit a lantern last night,
and relaxed out on my porch.

Revere Beach

I walk a beach out by Revere
And listen close to tidal flows,
The clouds all move to commandeer
I walk a beach out by Revere.
I see a soul so near appear
And walk a jetty the sea chose
I walk a beach out by Revere,
And listen close to tidal flows.

Through Maple Wood

My soul is troubled through the night
I walk in groves of maple trees,
A darkness grows inside my sight
My soul is troubled through the night,
I see emerging from the clouds
A full moons beauty, soft unease.
My soul is troubled through the night,
I walk in groves of maple trees.

The Sorrow of Artemis

He swam across the morning bay
She saw a dot afar,
"You can't hit that," he said, "No way!"
She aimed to shoot a star.
The goddess let the arrow loose
A thrum and thrip, it struck his juice,
The Goddess let the,
The Goddess let the,
Arrow rip her heart out of use.

He swam across the morning bay
She loved him with her heart,
Apollo had led her astray
His death rips her apart.
And Zeus will place him in the stars
Still chasing the Pleiades afar.
And Zeus will place,
And Zeus will place,
Orion up in nights lone jar.

He swam across the morning bay
His body floating in,
Poseidon rose so old and grey
The hunter pale as sin
Orion calls his dogs no more
And walks to Hades darker shore,
Orion calls his dogs,
Orion calls his dogs,
A ghost, a haunter on the moor.

Love is Fire

Love is fire of cherished faithful dreams,
As moonlit snow beneath maple trees show
A blue reflection of my souls extremes.

A hearts kindness that shows in glowing gleams
And warmth by tender hearths, to feel a glow
Love is fire of cherished faithful dreams,

To dance a waltz, so slow by moonlit streams
As beating hearts and pulsing rhythms know,
A blue reflection of my souls extremes;

In time the mortal tide shall pull our seams
Yet bring our hearts to never leave the flow,
Love is fire of cherished faithful dreams.

My love lay far across the seas and streams
A faith in something more, some lost plateau
A blue reflection of my souls extremes.

Yet standing here beneath soft moonlit beams
I search midnight for signs in stars to know,
Love is fire of cherished faithful dreams
A blue reflection, of my souls extremes.

The Stars Cross Above the Moor

I walked on out upon the darker moors, to think
Beneath the moon as Jupiter and Venus rose,
The smell of flora floats, as heath so sews a link.

By ancient bogs, a wisp of phantom air to wink
A woman caused a start, my mind so traced and froze,
I walked on out upon the darker moors, to think

She hadn't been, yet here she was, in shock I blink
Perfumes so lace in heath, enchanting charms arose
The smell of flora floats, as heath so sews a link.

A phantom girl so deep in moors, she spoke of mink
Yet here, her lover laid her body down, in woes
I walked on out upon the darker moors, to think

In darker waters, with the bogs she drowns in pink
Her sombre songs, of love reveal her fateful prose
The smell of flora floats, as heath so sews a link.

My mind, is wreathed and blue as fabric souls will drink
As she dissipates near morning, an east wind blows,
I walked on out upon the darker moors, to think
The smell of flora floats, as heath so sews a link.

Winter Rains

I breathe, as winter rain is falling melting snow
The air so coolly crisp and smell the chimney smoke,
Believe in shades of love, at times in fields aglow.

A gift of beauty, grace of God still lives to show
The heart of man has much to learn, a life awoke
I breathe, as winter rain is falling melting snow.

In fields and farms and dreams of wooded glens bestow
So full of birds in song as music softly spoke,
Believe in shades of love, at times in fields aglow.

As magic flows of spirit seek a truth, to know
Moments will lapse, of reason still, of faith evoke
I breathe, as winter rain is falling melting snow.

In vistas fair, of maple groves and winter flow
As sparrows perch in bushes near, my heart so woke.
Believe in shades of love, at times in fields aglow

To walk the pond and feel its life renew, I grow
As seeds of faith, will bury deep my heart so spoke,
I breathe, as winter rain is falling melting snow
Believe in shades of love, at times in fields aglow.

The Music of Fantasy

I Listen close to the choral music of night
In dreams so woven still of ancient streams, I sigh
In dark remains the cooler breath of winters height

So shimmers down the stars over hills snowy white
In nocturnes checked desires will burn and burn the sky,
I listen close to the choral music of night.

Enchanted spells will weave on through my heart on sight,
Of Beethoven's Helene Grimaud, my soul will fly.
In dark remains the cooler breath, of winters height

Enveloped near the spells of music sweetly light
My feelings run the spread of deeper darkly wry,
I listen close to the choral music of night.

In Grieg I see in shades and dream of darker flight
To hear the halls of where mountain kings reign, I cry.
In dark remains the cooler breath, of winters height

Peer Gynt, I would so wish to see the thrilling sight
A fantasy in dreams, a dreamers silent sigh
I listen close to the choral music of night,
In dark remains the cooler breath, of winters height.

The Ballad of the Ice Dragon

I dream of dragons high above
A dusty village keep,
The circling demon breathing ice
Will flood in winters sleep.

The dragon blue and venomous
Encased the keep in ice,
It was no use to calm the beast
For there we paid a price.

My love was then so taken by
The beast of mighty ice,
She went outside to ask of it
Of what would now suffice.

I dream of dragons high above
A dusty village keep,
The circling demon breathing ice
Will flood in winters sleep.

The dragon landed close to her
And spoke so to entice,
"I need of you so brave of heart
An elfin girl so nice."

She went away with the dragon
I watched her roll the dice,
The dragon flew with her so far
And magics sweet device.

I dreamed of dragons high above
A dusty village keep,
The circling demon breathing ice
Will flood in winters sleep.

The beast returned a day after
Encasing village thrice,
He saved me but for last to see
His phantom wings concise.

Alone in wastes of snowy white
I saw inside advice,
I raised my bow, flaming arrow
And shot the beast precise.

I dreamed of dragons high above
A dusty village keep,
The circling demon breathing ice
Will flood in winters sleep.

To my dismay the breath of life
So froze the shot in ice,
The anger curled inside the beast
And breathed upon me twice.

And then he took up to the sky
And left us all in ice,
Alone in fields of winter snows
A phantom world in ice.

I dreamed of dragons high above
A dusty village keep,
The circling demon breathing ice
Will flood in winters sleep.

On The Opening Act Of Sanctuary

The sky above is fair unclouded blue
So whispers winds of prayers and thoughts by day,
To live and walk so free of fear's cafe
A songbird singing three swift beats on cue
Out back beside the thicker trees he knew
Do you so feel the tensions building sway?
As songs a twit, a twit, a lee, away
So far a branch to hear his songs imbue.

I wonder where the sanctuary will go,
In Faulkner's tale a fate will darkly be
As chance to meet a foe by an old spring.

On deeper looks I see a form and flow
That Benbow dreams in curves of life, is free
In worlds of swirling thoughts and deeper swing.

The Flower Moon

The brighter moonlight washes out the sky
To see the beauty here by Eastern shore,
As the full flower moon, my eyes adore
And dreams of her will fill my hearts reply.

I watch the moon so trace across the night
As walking down the path around Rag Rock
A ghostly wood, to haunt my dreams and walk,
If only you were here, my dreams delight.

Yet here I know, I would go where you are.
I would still leave this hollow glen to see
A blessed heart, will pull my soul to be
My ragged pieces show beneath my scar.

Wild flowers dance in softer winds and light
I search to find an echo of your sight.

On Love
(A Sonnet Crown)

1

Of what is passing here but time, so time
Is ticking, ticking, ticking, though I live,
In finer style than before, I will to give
My passions still so wildly drift to chime
In bells, so ringing, ringing, ringing fine.
I cherish days and nights, to now relive
The sounds of joy my life has seen outlive,
my soul and here I know my mortal wine.

The steps of Saint Joseph's I held in care
Descending with my bride to waiting friends,
It was my happy life so long ago,
And seems to wait, a love of life so rare
About the home are flowers lush in blends,
To stave off moods of woven darker woe.

2

To stave off moods of woven darker woe
I sip a coffee brew and think of love,
It comes in flashes here to mind and shove
The darker dreams in flight, my spirits glow.
I seem to see a nicer way and know
It thrives on thoughts of tender warmth above,
So quiet now I wait and hear a dove
As light inside my soul, my hearts tableau.

My dreams are what I have so rent by mead,
It flows solvent in airy whims of fate,
In time, my soul so drinks of heavens light
So love, my love, as soon the path will lead
To home, to life and tender hearts of late
I lay my thoughts as wreathes, in sound delight.

3

I lay my thoughts as wreathes, in sound delight
As winter touches near my heart, I see
The boy I once had been, in solid glee
As days are short, I long for warmth and light,
So here my hearth in warming glows invite
A quiet soul to share the time, my key,
My life, my tender loving wife, my plea
To cast off darker plagues of soul tonight!

Yet, love is love and mine will brew for you
A tenderness of heart, a beacon gleams
In darken groves of trees in painted rows,
Be still the dream, a stream of light I drew
We dance by lights enfolding loving beams,
To draw on grace, a feeling surely glows.

4

To draw on grace, a feeling surely grows
In joy and laughter, hearts will beat as one,
As you I see along the path we run
Before I sleep, and when I wake, I know
In tender ways, the years begin to sow,
But though I grey, in age my line has none
So when you dance in winds, my hearts undone,
My love, my sweetest rose, in wreaths of clothes.

So here I show my thoughts of love to keep
The dark at bay, as light the feeling warms,
My lantern glows amid the snowy downs
And cheers us long and timeless years of sleep,
As storms are weathered here, we know the norms
So still we form the bonds of timeless crowns.

5

So still we form the bonds of timeless crowns
Away the show, alight by mortal dawn,
I am but yours, and yours alone so drawn
Of you, I see your flowing tress and gowns,
My dreams of you in these will chance the rounds.
Remember days of youth in art redrawn
We hold the light of joy, in each a fawn,
So cast in marble stands the soul of sounds.

Yet, still I speak my heart on love and life
Enchanting forms of feelings I bestow,
I speak of her as love, my darling wife
My soul in love, my heart is all I know.
A music plays in through the trees of strife
We dance in groves of hushing sweet willow.

6

We dance in groves of hushing sweet willow
By breezes swiftly sweeping past us clear,
As snowy drifts enshrouding sweetly near
In warm embrace, we keep a tender glow.
My deepest wish, a dream of you, I know
Has drawn out long, a train of years and years,
As there began a life, so thread the gears
And thrust the pedal down, a pace below.

As thoughts of you so lace my mortal mind
Recalling dreams I knew along the path,
In you, I see the honest love and want.
A tender thrill of time so here refined
As models drawn by art, we draw a bath
We soak the many nights, of old Vermont.

7

We soak the many nights, of old Vermont
The cottage life we have and sweet relief,
As love, so heals the wounds and steals the grief.
My life is here complete, I have no want
In passions breathe the winds of starker fonts
I hold in you desire of high belief
And sate my thirsting mind along the reef,
The sails of barks at sea adrift in want.

As hand in hand we have each single day
To drift eternal tides of graceful time,
Of days, of nights we have enough to share
In you, my love has known no bounds to say
and pausing here by scenes of snow sublime,
I know no other soul, as love is rare.

Nonsense and Tea

I'm not sure if I should be the one, to say this
As I think, you are quite a bit stranger of late.
So as you may be thinking of rhyme and bodice
I've a mind to try laughter instead, so ornate
Imagine you are wondering what to dismiss
As humor is so tricky, my rhymes will deflate.

And I'll send you a package too soon by airfreight
So you wonder if yanks can be witty princess?
As I've chosen an odd meter here to vibrate
A bit rare, a tad dim, as it feels so amiss
I had said, "as we Yanks do not drink tea," notate
A bit later, we threw it off ships, did we miss?

I now think my humor is all soft as a plank
As I crack a smile, I am still a dull yank.

In Fields of Daffodils

My heart is moved in meadows windy sway
In daffodils fair yellow hue, sweetly
Bowing with tulips flowing completely;
I feel the beauty in your words, so fey.

Your smile brims to fizzing warmly sweet
Beneath the boughs of the maples shading,
I loose sense, in tender dreams cascading
And feel the friendship blossom so complete.

Yet still the beauty calls in floras field
Refreshing souls with love and tenderness,
I'd dance beneath the moon, if you fluoresce
And move then these feelings, heartfelt I yield.

An old and shady tree, whose shelters give
The warmth of friends to circle close and live.

Spring's Garden

As daffodils in bloom
Begin to paint my yard
The subtle tones perfume
The gardens yellow bard
A fair and sunny guard
To sweep the blues and gloom.

Irises sprouting near
And crocus blooming soft
So splash the colors clear
In winds tulips so waft
As gentle fragrant soft
A meadow garden here.

A garden built by Spring
Can cause a heart to sing.

In Fantasia's Sketch

I walked along a fairy meadow path
as bees and butterflies flutter and buzz,
my swooning mind in swirling lazy sways
my stroll, a sing-song voice or rhythmic bath.
Yet, here along the trail my spirits fuzz
electric like a ripened peach ablaze,
so stirs my pot and moving time in wrath.
To quiet life in evening calm because
I could in breathing deeply stir, my rays
of sun to shine along the sprites of Kath.

So still on perching rocksby meadow brook
a quickly darting nymph of gossamer,
as she so coyly peeks around the nook
afleeting glimpse, aswift moss reclaimer.

The Heated Room

Sunlight still filters muted through fabric
Of curtains drawn and formless keeping heat
Humid air tinges sticky skin as slick
And beading drops of sweat begin to cheat.
The roomis baking like a steam bath brick
As dimmer light of late day fades complete
The songs of birds are ripe and lush on wicks
Of tree and scrub, yet here I feel off-beat.

The room is like a vault, still faintly breathes
As clothing clings to tacky skin, I wait
As finer drops of dewy sweat drip down
I mop my face and wade in steamy wreaths
Releasing dreams of winter nights ornate
As snow descends to wither here and drown.

The Price

I look outside as birds buzz through the air
The clouds still swirling darkly overhead,
The storm's electric wrath still building flair
As roiling elementals see despair.

The depth of waiting catches hold in dread
As wraiths of times immortal rise return,
For children born of Cain, the earth has fed
Of Abel's blood in ghosts of those undead.

In realms we dare not see the tides have spurned
And freed ancient demons to feast on souls,
As time vanquished on Cain an endless burn
A brother's face to see again and yearn.

Who knows the weight on Cain, the price he tolls
The vagabond of winter's reaching shoals.

The Songs of Night

The stars in bloom on summer nights revive
A wandering and idle mind, to breathe
In deep and sweeter breaths of air, survive
And keep the night, to live, to laugh, to seethe.

So how is there enough to lay one's self
Upon the floor of straw, of dust to sleep?
Nature so rests upon the hazy shelf
So pure and sweet in veils of dreams we keep.

My thoughts so trace the stars in lines of dots,
Across skyward canvases draw demure
And fairer lines of finer grains of blots,
Lion, a snake, a turtle's form allure.

Inhaling visions leading to Zion
And through the wooded glens, drifting ion.

The Iron Gate

I watch arrows flowing through goldenrod
A thwump! A twang! Released 'em from the bow,
Inside the swaying yellow fields, they glide
The ghostly showers flitter through the sod;
Surprising sounds of wounded souls below
Arise up from the hollow, wilder side.

Lilacs of cottage gardens dream abroad
In rows of hostas flourish creamy shows,
Beneath the morning glory wreaths untied
I walk in through the lilies flowing nod;
A listless strolling garden, dreams in-tow
I saunter here on mosses long astride.

I watch the flowing goldenrod in rain
Inside the garden gates, I now remain.

Ripples

To dream in modes of Celtic frost and breathe
A breath as steam exhaling, pauses thought
To wonder here or there, to rant and seethe
Of dreams or thoughts impure, I stand distraught.

My winter changes now to spring, a thaw
To melt remaining snow, as crocus blooms
In dabs of garden blush and swift guffaw,
In smiles painted lips enhance perfumes.

Enchanted here idling, a butterfly
So softly flutters dreaming softly still,
To bathe on sunlit rocks as William Bligh
The whispers turn to wake a stirring thrill.

I seem to pass beneath the dreams reply
and wade inside the rippled waves of why.

In Songs of Winter

Rhythms of swirling, roiling snow silently falls
On wooded glens, around the ponds and lakes
Descending graceful puffs of downy flakes,
My spirit wanders near, enclosed in shawls
Of wonder here, my faithful mind recalls.
The timeless scenes are beautiful and makes
My path and tread so pause in searching shakes
To watch the stormy skies in waiting drawls.

But here, my feet are growing cold and damp
I seem enchanted gazing deep in thought,
Yet here I am, so cold as shivers seep;
To watch the world lay claims of fluffy vamp
And steal the grains of sand and coldly wrought
My soul in purest rays of joy, to keep.

R. Tirrell Leonard Jr.

The Cooper Hawk

Awaking early morn I went to place
A pot to boil water, then I saw
The Cooper Hawk in wait, I was in awe.
It twitched its head and moved about to trace
The boughs and trees for signs of food. It cased
My yard and turned silently spread and yawed
Above the frozen land in chase of law,
A jay or wren, it soared after in space.

The wren or blue jay wove around the homes
In through encrusted, frozen trees pursued,
A hawk of stealth, a pretty raptor flew
And heaved along urban intrepid domes;
As whistles steam, the kettle grabs me shrewd,
The path of predator and prey imbue.

Pausing Near The Winter Woods

The whispered winds so stir the snowy downs
As passing here I pause in haunting wood,
To hear the moaning stir of branch, I stood
In depths of drift beneath the starry crowns.
In dreams of beauty, breathe enchanted sounds
I reel as roiling snow in tendrils would,
As sighs escape my lips and lift the hood
I feel the seeping cold in ghostly rounds.

Ah, yet I shall not want the breath of snow
Or whitish slopes and frozen fields to warm,
As melting here along the scene and gone;
And dreams of summer shall so sing to show
In swirls of color painting fields transform,
To grasp my soul in swoons of mortal dawn.

R. Tirrell Leonard Jr.

The Scarlet Letter

A rose of tender value grows so near
In purity its value shows so pure,
It seems to live and thrive in holy fear
As within spells of darken fate demure.
A solid door of black iron was wrought,
To tell a tale of humble tones, so cold
As she so lightly steps away distraught,
Her guilt is not alone by ways of old.
So taken here of darken tempest hate
A cross is bourn and breaks a tender rose,
The ghastly wretched scene so bound the soul
Auspice so grim and comes austere her fate
A vow on heaven's soil sought by those
Of harsh silence absent of sweet console.

I close my eyes to dream of you, so near
In roiling thoughts so vanishing in mists,
I see a wintry dream so clothed, my dear
As ice envelops trees and snow persists.

The world is rent in shades of winter white
My mind is far away in biting cold,
Encased in reams of ice, no living light
To see the wasted lands, a province told.

So haunted dreams will scream to knights and trolls
In sweat so drenched my thoughts, to see a life,
And scatter all the leaves beneath the coal
As coldness steals the warmth, in living strife.

To dream of you so close will soothe my heart,
As fondness warms the spirits that depart.

A Journey

The journey here, is mine to bring about
As huckleberry bushes line my sight,
Of reaching branches shading here despite
The notion holds in cups of palms devout
To see a spring so freshly sprung, and stout
To breathe in air of deeper rich twilight;
Is sense and wit to differ here at night?
Ah beauty, such is life in this . . . I doubt.
Yet here, my mind shall veer off beat and path
And hold my hands outstretched before the rain,
For hope is all, so all I need is here.
A long and riddled trek is drenched in wrath
As here it dies in muddied toil, to gain
So, what became the man of honest cheer?

The Werewolf's Moon

I lay awake inside a waking night
In pools of sweat, my terror bursts in screams
An avatar so reels distorting fright,
A bell so struck in deep resounding streams
To pry on fears of longing, gnashing teeth . . .
On wasted lands demarcation, I seethe
A rage of boiling, fiery anger flows
My bodies changeling form of cursed and damned,
I am the wolf by moons delight below
And hunted hence as night to day, has slammed.
Yet, time has changed again in barren lands
As red my eyes by tidal moon bequeaths.

The change is stilled in death as blood remands
A timeless fallen wretch, my life has spanned.

The Long Walk

As sun so bakes the still of day, it came
A wall of smoke invades the land in fear
A sound so moiled the earth, on hoofs aflame,
As through the noise, a blue man rose to leer.
Kit Carson rode in burning fields of corn,
The Utes so helped in carnage here, to claim
As roiling smoke in tendrils rose a scorn
The Navajo and lands so rent in shame.
Surrender came on broken winds of war
As thieves in blue escort the tribe away
Eight thousand walked along the ruins and gore,
The darkest fort so waits for their dismay.

In costly tides of sand, so walk the dead
As many lives are lost along the thread.

The Dark Veil

Rain falling softly in the rain
restrains a subtle voice restrained
caress softly hushing caress
impress upon me, to impress.

So rents my fabric mind, just so
flows a murky water, in flows.
Bequest, a stranger dark bequest
impress upon me, to impress.

Yet, hues are not blended just yet
forget in spells and then forget.
Bless the souls, and inside you bless
impress upon me, to impress.

Rain falling softly in the rain
impress upon me, to impress.

The Russian Winter

Retreat was shouted loud, in storms of men
Russians fell back, so burn the fields to char
The grand army had all but won, till then.
In scorched and blackened earth, by fallen bars
The downy flake began to fall, so to
A wintry wrath has skulked the avatar.
On frozen plains of ice and snow, a zen
So blankets soldiers, fiery, cold, and far.
To home and warmth of yet to starve, but when
A barren waste, the earth had seemed to mar
The empty void of ruined fields often
had felt death hunting the dying shelters.

The frozen souls, vacant in eyes so lost
The earth was still to hear silence of cost.

Winter Chill

Inside my dream has drowned, to wrench below
the moving tides, as tender warmth so fades.
A fabric mind afloat in fluids flow
to change my course, to move my soul in spades.
As frosty etched and frozen glass aglow
of light mirrored by ice, in cold cascades.
So winter comes at last to this chateau,
its frosty breath has wheezed, in winds betrayed
by moaning trees, so cold beneath the snow.
As silken curves rapture on winds remade
of snowy dunes so deeply lush, bestows
my soul, a sight and thought, of dreams decayed.

A dream beneath a filling moon so howls
in minds of mortal men, in winter's jowls.

The Tolling Bells

The knell of brass bells rings my faith askew,
It has silenced the plague, and squandered land
In darkened rooms of Salem halls, pursues
A writ against the pure of faith to brand.

So closed a book of heavy weight, and breath
Its leather smell of older days ignites,
A soul so lost as light recedes, oh death!
As time so ticks away unearthly night.

The judge has snuffed the candle out on life
Its smoky tendrils waft to silence souls
In thunderous vex slam the book on strife,
The darkened oak awaits my neck and foal.

So ring the bells, and slam the holy book,
To cast a man far from the saintly brook.

A Thought In Hand

I hold a thought sitting so near the shore
In hands so bruised by work, I search the trees,
Rising up from the muddy rocks, it bore
A muse on budding limbs of oak so free.

As curious fowl arrive at my scene
I stand up now and wandering so near,
(It may be when the thought was born and weaned)
As life so took a hold of ghostly fear.

I hold it now and turn it in my mind
a score of thoughts in blooming timely might,
So would I change my fabric life in kind,
A softer sound caressing swelling light?

I share my life, to know my soul's desire
In darkness soft, enfolds a bodies fire.

In Stream

I have often in thought on self-preserve,
A sort of leaky roof, not sealed or tight.
It may occur to senses swift of nerve
As thoughts as mine, on these muses of light.
Or, has my mind a thrumming vice, nor curve
As light on mirrors, falls infinite, right?
To days of light and dark, tensions will swerve
About the tides, in rain or playing slight.

Yet, dark partakes the drink in golden cups
As sullen strains of vices, reaching thrice
In pulling matter full in view of dice,
So rolled, so rolled, as strong as little mice.
I've seen in flashes, lightning moving up
As thoughts so plain on fabric walls entice.

Cold Hours

December weighs so heavy, worn or free
its grace entraps my soul in falling snow,
the veils of whitish, fluffy, falling flake
so sets my heart, of sad visions to see.
The bare elm branches lined, on paths aglow
in icy rims refracting stars opaque
and gilded light, so stirring realms to flee—
I pray to God up high, and hope will show
a world of beauty, kindly graced awake.
So bathed in light and warmth, of storms debris
and wrapped about the waist, in blankets flow
as frost encroaches windowpanes, in cakes
I have so fallen here, by shrouds of hope
to weave in life wintry wreaths, to cope.

Scream

So with the dream, so lifts my mind and life,
a trouble caused inside my weaving sight
is drifting rough, infinite streaming time.
A falling soul, so calls to God in line
as whispers trace the fabric silken light,
the reams and shards, of glass comply in strife.
A great expanse of sky or sea, by knife
to separate the names, divine design.

I pour my balm over my fears, my dreams
to walk instep, imbued by sole belief,
and still my ears, of hearing lucid screams
of long so tired nights, solace, relief,
I lay my quaking bones, in realms of streams.
A dust to settle, breaks the roles of grief.

The Hours That Pass

In waking here, beneath the changeling boughs
my heart wanders though, along this brook,
In dreaming I took my mind, but away
to whimsy's grasp, sways my sinking soul—free!

So the tonic, seething pain abridged such woes
to pour out although, it wrought the drugged rooks
so surly forsook, this rotting decay.

Of what misdeed, preys upon my mind, be
as with simple trees along the shore? So
a wretch yet crowed, "A struggle for crooks!"
And, "Let the people hook issues of the day!"

In flimsy limbs swaying, for worlds to see,
as it will all rewind, like soil to sow
of tomorrow's woes steeped in cups of tea.

The Rising King

A gift arrives beneath a winters tree
Adorned by mantles of powerful age,
So crowned by sages, elves, and normal folks.
He seems to say the rightful things, to be
In this his knowledge tells of hidden rage,
To quench a thirst at once, to break the yolks!
If freedoms plight has been plundered at sea,
Is there still room, in the silence of stage?
The call of wilderness, magic invokes.
A chanting rhythm stills a knight's decree
To fight the realms of darkness that engage,
A souls enchanted strength, still found in oaks.

If eagles soar up high, is this a gift
To see, to witness gliding swift—adrift?

The Tiny Hord

Withering winds wist through the darkening trees
In color shades of gold, orange, or red,
The Goldenfinch's song, so whistles with glee
So bathes in sunlight kisses overhead.
Autumnal rustic cheer, of pumpkins spread
Over the countryside boroughs and ponds,
A feeling growing, speeding fate responds
Orchards ripening with appealing dread.

So soothing candy in many a pouch
Costumed pirates, witches, fairies and ghost,
Arrive in droves along byways to crouch
To leave a little sweeter, each one boasts!
Of settling handouts, sugary sweet slouch
Appears every small child around the coast.

Dawn

A thrill ran through my soul
so truth be told, my eyes befell
a tragic depth if hunger sate,
of feasted blood all through the night.
My soul, so chill aside in waning light,
enfolds a mist of white.

The shrill sparrow's song sings, at dawn
in plain and misty air,
by fir, by pine, by subtle brook
near juniper, oaks, and birch.
A sullen song on bloodless wings
clings vapor tendrils of this spring.

A thrill ran through my soul,
the shrill sparrows song sings, at dawn.

Castle Walls

Now within mist enfolding walls I see
The castle rising from the white vapor
It grieves the dark, beneath the reaching trees.

So sets the fret-cut teeth, to doom scraper
In scratching jest! It haunts the scarce banshee
So lost, in ways intent, urgent, graaper

Idyllic charms of blessings, fell my eyes
In blending haze of sun in fog she walked
A graceful lady stirred me to arise.
The signs became a gull as hunting stalked.

Reddish hellfire so bloomed in either glance
As visions kept her haunting me in trance,
My gloom resumed besetting for a spell
Yet here beneath a calling lark, I dwell.

Into The Hush Of Night

Stirs the cricket chirping lively and bright
beneath the lush clouds of evening's beauty,
a solace to a midnights stroll is here
within the cleaner air of phantom night.
A woman found by my gaze, a cutie
slender, curvy, in fashion styled to sear—
Has my attention slipped? No! I am fine.
But, my reverie has settled booty
ah! That is mans mind, to dream her rear
morning, noon, it's nice; much like a good wine
supple, graceful, elegant her many facets.
So dreams the spell and sips of her unclear.

My emotion stirs evening's tender climb,
to contemplate her nurturing assets.

Morph

So winter reaches thus, my fairy queen
has leapt up from the leaves and grass to fly.
Aloft the airy foams of spring, so shy
As spells of magic weave the fabric scene.

A wrinkle in the cloth of time, a cry
of soft caress and fragrant dreams to weld
the metal fabric souls in blends so held
in high regards across the lands and sky.

The bark has bled along as trees rebelled,
unseen by those along idyllic roads.
So mark the spells swirling in faster modes,
a plan to bring the boys to home, upheld.

So withers magic from the fraying peace,
as lost and lonely are the dying sheep.

In Thundering Snows

A shattered rough, Nature so threw my sense
in awe observed the fall of snow, I watched
as quick the lightning struck out from the storm
the chillso bleakly shown, a thunderhead.

So gave my pulse a rise, to thinkof whence
andlent to beautyflowing thoughts so notched.
A life remembers, lost in timeless form
of sweet lamenting dreams, so left unsaid.

The clouds so black as coal, elect offence
as sweet the tides of snow descending botched
a view so feint, a traithumanly warm.
Onwhich of these, before thedrawto bed

the thoughts of mine so rest the dream of life,
before the grace of thunderingsnows, strife.

Moonlight Reverie

I sit along the water's edge watching
the darkening tides beginrolling in,
as the quiet pale moonlight shivers still
upon caressing early evening waves.

Nogallant screams, from the lurking seagulls
circling over, for a fast food handout.
life takes no notice of an empty beach,
I hear beneath the moonlit tides, a sea.

My mind traces the crowds at day, to roam
along the narrows, where the poor men stroll.
In lines for soup and bread, a meal that's hot.
Served by thankless good souls, distilled in time.

The water laps greedily the loose sand
remembering cradlesrocking so unplanned.

Dreaming In Myths

Ulysses rising from the soot
in silver robes left underfoot,
while softer rains fall to the earth
the wicked tames his golden mirth.

A legend that his servant told
has since grown mosses ages old,
a temper marked by mighty girth
the wicked tames his golden mirth.

Avalon seen by star swept seas
immortal reigns a softer breeze;
legends give us a quiet berth
the wicked tames his golden mirth.

Ulysses rising from the soot
the wicked tames his golden mirth.

Thistle Rush

The honeyed lilt of voice, so sweetly sang
across the tides of sea swept souls, she calls.

So soft is her feline embrace, and form
as rounded in her flesh, to burn and clang.

To moods, our hearts unite and supple falls
as heavenly bodies clash, and transform.

My mind has raced over the ebbing tides
and knows her soul, like mine warmly resides.

Her nipples trace my chest, and loose my mind
devours my soul, in waves of greedy fire.

As my thoughts engage, her fleshy hot cage
her lips linger, over my skin, to grind.

An age of lust and longings quenched, in choir
I held her softened curves and mortal rage.

Winter Sparrows

I watch the sparrows feed, upon the tree
A tallow cake, to swarm and sing alight;
As winter storm, suspends the chills of rain.
The snows full weight, beneath the old banshee
As she screams in mists, a frozen shrill blight.
The tree so meek, the sparrows call remains
In merry laughter, it seems to breathe so free
Resounds the tones of idler springs, so bright!

The spell of winter woven myth, retains
A moldy book, so worn its yellowed page.
As songs a sparrow sings, of light refrain,
Remind the passerby, the storms full rage.
Still I watch, in the mix of winter pains
As back the snow returns, my idle gage . . .

Immortal Chains

I heard her calling, over star swept seas
My dreams of lust, so burned my bones
And left my body, writhing to atone
For darkened chambers, locked to me
The flames so licked my flesh, enclosed alone;
To walk so chaste, the wind bemoans,
As Ghostly steps enchants, the hearts to thee!
Set aside such thrust, this wretch, was once me.

To fly in myths, my feet are quite off ground
As this soul's afire, of gasoline dreams
I have but ceased to be, yet chained and bound;
Enclosed by the humming river, I seam
But sullen in my later moods, and sounds
Alarm of rapture, to quench dry parched reams.

B

Betwixt

The swell of tides, thus came upon her dress
Captured her heart, as darkness wept, for love.
The long an darker blight, of her, a dove.
"So Pip," she said, "you came to heart, confess."
The blade of steel, so cuts the deep of bone
An severs hearts an souls, devours the shame.
The fire so licked the flesh of time's leg lame,
And ushered cold, a lonely hearts cyclone.

The page so lifts a spirit now, foreseen
As grim the doctor's wrathful ways, obscure
Grimshawe and great expectations, between
Two great writers, of stinging dark allure.
Hawthorne and Dickens bring so forth, the fire.
Exposing societies wroth dim sire . . .

A truce I call, upon the darkened veil.
A hand so said to move the tides so well.
Victim of society's fears, so sails
A day of storms, I knew, forgive me belle?
As time so weeps into the porous sand
My hours dwindle wroth, as the shade so moves
To clear a name? Nay, for the sun commands
My head to bow to this blow, my soul soothed.

As I leave these native soils, I forgive
Of those, so jealous souls, I had once known.
As they so eat a dish, of humble pie
I smile to know, it torments the sieves
And writhes in their mischief, to walk alone.
My soulso born of tougher sod retries . . .

Voices call across the sea, to my ears
the fallen leaves rustle, 'neath the chill east wind,
all blessings, that befall my mortal eyes.

So breathes, in this dream, as hot drought of wine,
while the chill of winters wroth touch, my fears
expel with steam, as parting lips, rescind—

Warble of the bluebirds song, sweetly flies
unto my listening ears! Supple vines
Oh, Halcyon days, gone by . . . Who sheds tears?

Over the false beliefs, bereft of night,
Who profits? As Johnny came marching home,
awful darkness, his winter washed ashore—

What sullen days retold, again for blight?
Our hero walks, a barren wasteland's loam—

Oh! Radiant visages of beauty stay
so near, to this Irish heart of desire,
as eyes of sparkling and dazzling may
ignite this passions promise afire.

A giddy feeling quells deep this bosom,
as fashioned in this clay mill, sweet union.
Softly, waxing its toll, my souls blossom,
as our friction embroils our communion.
I shudder beneath the crush of embrace
and yearn to be, of that communal force,
to torch my soul in your gasoline lace
to melt inside of you, my souls divorce.

As breathlessly left beneath your splendor,
unchaste desires want, of you I adore.

Cascade of dreams, so lives my heart aflame
As water so trembles over my soul,
A gentle slumber holds me firm cajole.
Her subtle form ignites her curves reclaim,
enfolds me within her vortex of fire.
As your nails trace my lines heated luster;
So bind my hands in fiery flesh, so flustered;
and rake your nails, in torrid, urgent desire.

So nestle wanton, within our embrace,
and dream to whet hot, this sated hunger;
to feel this burning unquenchable thirst.
So purge my longings of the night encased
to rage volcanic heart, a melted monger . . .
So wrap my thoughts in bed, to yearn immersed . . .

Crusader

My fate resides but last, inside my mind
is withering, as autumn leaves of trees.
So chaste, it breathes a rank desperate sound
that lay awake inside the waxing night.

So when I gaze on winter's arid sea,
with eyes of flesh and stone, so cold and blind.
To sate my hunger on this storm of fright
and burn alive this lust, yet spurned unbound.

So chain me down to this darkened blight,
yet echoes since the days, crusades so crowned;
and separate lots of scorned desire flee
to distant battles left to dust and time . . .

Denied that flesh of contact supple fire,
consigned to fate, blood lust rebels desire.

Wanton my eyes drink her in lustily
her supple curves ignite my souls desire
on sheets of silken dreams I surrender.

So sate my lust on such bliss artfully
enfold me in your forms eternal fire
look upon your body, coy splendor.

To whet this old-mans dreams so completely . . .
You rack my body rake the coals entire,
so let mercy fall from your supple lips.

Enfold me in your dreams of heated flesh,
as I so twist, a feather inside wind;
submerged within you I am lost, eclipse . . .

Your legs enfold me with your arms enmeshed
lay me low, with your burning grace chagrined . . .

Boston Light

Sunrise at Brewster Isle, ignites my soul
glistening off the baying tides stately;
As the fog cannon, stands ready to sound.

Here upon this island, I could stroll
my thoughts linger to history lately,
for this is one of Boston's hidden gems.

To John Hancock, I give my praise unbound
for this light of graceful beauty cajoled;
while keeping the harbor safe innately . . .

Inspiring dreams laced romantic surround
the mariners go past with their sails hem,
to gaze upon the distant reach, to home.

Her decadence welcomes weary fishermen,
their hearts of joy, upon her sight—to roam . . .

R. Tirrell Leonard Jr.

The Fall Of Lal

Legends fall from grace as some fade away
This is with the story of Lal, vanished
Along with the times of dragons banished
Truss bridges connected the tree chalets.
As the day broke ominous over Lal
The dragons flew quietly on attack,
The truss bridges burned, the village was sacked;
Lone, a sentry stood, while dragons corral
The tarmac blackened in the dark scorched earth,
A vibrant village in the trees now burned
High in the redwood trees the sentry felt
The eyes of the dragonsgauging his worth,
Their talons he could see, as their breath churned
And the ice blue dragon flew near, he knelt . . .

Siege

Night has fallen upon my feeble mind
As my spirit bleakly speaks of the shade,
My eyes do seem to justify this blade
As it is unsheathed, glimmering, yet blind;
Somber edges blend weary wolves entwined
Like political foxes on crusades;
The hobgoblin press has been overplayed,
As the hours delay and the stars aligned
My tired self, I have taken to rest
While the problems untangle into a thought,
I find, I'm not much further on this course;
As heaven puts me to task and then test,
I file through pages of Plato, I bought
The sun rises painting a moral force.

To Braggers

I pray before the tribe and fall affront
my thoughts are lost to me, so here I stand
a trial rages within, storms my soul
deliver here the morrow dark and blunt.
In books before the world I state my brand
and dreams of what will come of sweet cajole,
so short my sights and lofty goals I punt
to quell vibrations shuttering demand.
Unbound my tongue and loose my lips extol
but here before the altered house of God
to lay a wreath on older ways, for chance
I care not now to know the morrows dog,
and called attentions to my faults advance
although, I seize the fans of flaming sod.

Softly Cries The Loon

My heart so yearns, the moon to rise regaining night
My soul yet burns, to dance beneath the pale full moon
As time adjourns, I see fair colors sway my sight
My mind so churns, beauty I witness softly croons.
Yet, softly on my turns, so twirls the beach tonight
A gentle whisper near returns, my sighs so soon
In sweet concerns, I feel his lift and spirit bright
I dance, as raining burns my inner self of boons.
A jig so spurns, about the beach in veils of light
And in the stars, my yearns are drowning sprigs in tune
So whispers softly earns and sorrows wrap the night
My love so blooms as wild ferns, as I hear the loon.
I feel my soul returns, as the loon calls tonight
The stars entwine concerns beneath the beauty moon.

R. Tirrell Leonard Jr.

On The Marginal Way

I wait for you, as sun shines down and warms my soul
A bench and view, of the sea whispers softly still
Yet here renews my faith, in all of life's goodwill
As seagulls soar above, My thoughts of you cajole.
The sounds of rolling waves against the shore console
Still beats my heart as noon flows past, I wait uphill
I search the faces on the path for you until
The sun dips down so rosy red and there you stroll.

Yet life has ways, to warm our hearts and minds to love
And waiting here on seaside bench, I want only
You near me, Thoughts and dreams remind us still, to live.
As on the Marginal Way, walking with you dove
My soul so thanks the lord, as we are not lonely
As anywhere with you is home, my love I give.

The Ballad Of Omar

Alone in fields of winter snows
A phantom world of ice
The cold has torn my love away
I search for wise advice.

A man who walked the barren plains
A dark wizard commands
His penetrating gaze to warm
Omar the man who stands.

The hunter melts in magic heat
He sinks in woes demands
Omar so longs to find his love
To hunt ice dragon lands.

Alone in fields of winter snows
A phantom world of ice
The cold has torn my love away
I search for wise advice.

Omar the hunter met the man
The rags fell rent by hands
The wizard met his icy gaze
"I hunt the dragon lands."

"I offer help in finding beasts
The winds of snows expands."
Omar agreed to track the fiend
Still on the barren lands.

Alone in fields of winter snows
A phantom world of ice
The cold has torn my love away
I search for wise advice.

His dreams are rent in bitter balms
In frozen meadow-lands
Before his eyes, the world is dark
To trek in snows soft brands.

A ghostly girl of ages past
Who stole his heart in lands
In days before the dragon came
His soul, now lost in sands.

Alone in fields of winter snows
A phantom world of ice
the cold has torn my love away
I search for wise advice.

In Murmurings Through Trees

Rainy days, will leave me thinking darkly.
How I hardly watch the rain so falling
Guarding thoughts of beauty still and starkly
Feeling wet beneath the trees, I'm scrawling
Slushing, sloshing, feelings fill me squalling
Yet I feel a music lightly strolling.
Hearing split and splish or sploshing calling
Branches through the sounds of rain so scrolling
Skies with lightning flashes bright and brawling
Fill my mind with wonders still and stalling.

Morning Cuppa

A fog is sitting with my mind
For coffee dreams or tea will wake
My soul so stirs the lemon rind
A fog is sitting with my mind
As beans will move inside a grind
And steaming, tasting soon forsake
A fog is sitting with my mind
For coffee dreams or tea will wake.

Shards of Light

Laced in through my dreams lay
Darker visions in layers
Lightning fills my souls sway
Laced in through my dreams lay
Songs and hymns of faiths way
Hear the cries inside prayers
Laced in through my dreams lay
Darker visions in layers.

R. Tirrell Leonard Jr.

Hunted

My footstep falls through snowy veils
as chills rip through my bones
like daggers made of ice and glass
my vision sees the shade at last.

A pale rider on a pale horse
a dark cloak bound her figure
death is a lady not kept waiting.

My last thoughts surrender
on the drifts of winds and snows.

She Searches

She sails the sea of crystal calms
to search for love, her true lone dove
on branches of the crimson palms
She sails the sea.

Beneath the stars, she finds the balms
she searches for true, lasting love
she rejoices and sends out alms.

Her mirth, full of laughter's sweet charms
She sails on moonlit tides thereof
For true loves course, can sway the psalms
She sails the sea.

Time stirring in the woods I walk
The crunching leaves, so softly mock
A cool wind rustles down the path
My thoughts wander towards Antioch.
Alexander's city so hath
The trading power's shining wrath
On Eastern shores of Orontes
So soon the winter shares the path.
The fall began invasions tests
And withers trading routes to bless
The jewel so loses now the light
A decline of ages contests.

I walk the woods and dream of night
The moon above the rivers height
In time, a still and soaring kite
In time, a still and soaring kite.

On Jetty's By The Sea

If you were queen of Venus
And I man of Titan
I'd cross the cosmic distance
With regular persistence
We'd walk beaches of Malvinas
There love shall enlighten;
If you were queen of Venus
And I man of Titan.

If you were a girl of Mars
And I boy of Saturn
I'd bring you the planet's rings
And dream softly as you sing
We'd sail across cosmic stars
Tracing fabric pattern;
If you were a girl of Mars
And I boy of Saturn.

If wishes flew to the stars
And you were here with me
We'd see the coastal beaches
In life the world yet teaches
And forget about our scars
On jetty's by the sea;
If wishes flew to the stars
And you were here with me.

If you were queen of Venus
And I man of Titan
I'd cross the cosmic distance
With regular persistence
We'd walk beaches of Malvinas
There love shall enlighten;
If you were queen of Venus
And I man of Titan.

Capricorn

Starlight so draws my brown eyes
A whisper escapes lips
My soul is impressed above
Like my search for my sweet dove
Hours breath so softly replies
Rain on oaks as dew drips;
Starlight so draws my brown eyes
A whisper escapes lips.

Dark seas draw my soul to stir
On jetty's breach I wait
Salt sweet air I love to taste
Awaiting sunrise so traced
Horizons breath will concur
Stars softly sing of fate;
Dark seas draw my soul to stir
On jetty's breach I wait.

In nighttime woods I'm at peace
Roam the path wooded knolls
Moonlight peaks through branches bare
I feel phantoms in their care
Fabric years of sweet caprice
Realms where shadow tolls;
In nighttime woods I'm at peace
Roam the path wooded knolls.

Starlight so draws my brown eyes
A whisper escapes lips
My soul is impressed above
Like my search for my sweet dove
Hours breath so softly replies
Rain on oaks as dew drips;
Starlight so draws my brown eyes
A whisper escapes lips.

Twilight Sighs

So I listen close to dreams
And close my eyes and sigh
My love is but a flower
Enfolding me with power
Drawn upon the mystic streams
Laid up on shores to cry;
So I listen close to dreams
And close my eyes and sigh.

So I listen to meadows
And feel the breath of life
The warming sun upon me
Cardinals songs guarantee
Warmer winds will surely blow
And end the looming strife;
So I listen to meadows
And feel the breath of life.

So I listen to sad songs
Tinged with a light called hope
So sewn in dreams of beauty
Aching swift sullen booty
My heart to the night, belongs
A sullen mess to mope;
So I listen to sad songs
Tinged with a light called hope.

So I listen to night winds
And pray to feel at ease
It rattles the maple leaves
Softly traces all my grieves
Alone a feeling rescinds
In darkness I so freeze;
So I listen to night winds
And pray to feel at ease.

As I listen to silence
And wish I was not here
I drink upon a whirlwind
Lost in a mad maze of hymn
Timbres ring inside silence
Resounding cool frontier;
As I listen to silence
And wish I was not here.

Still I listen to the moon
And hear her twilight sighs
A river flowing swiftly
Falling, a leaf blows alee
Hearts are broken jewels, so strewn
I hear a soul who cries;
Still I listen to the moon
And hear her twilight sighs.

Morning

In the morning, the sparrows sing
and wake my bones from their nights rest
the songs and rhythms these hymns bring
In the morning.

A feeling here I must attest
as trees fizz, in the winds of Spring
A feeling grows, to live as blessed.

Remember taking to a swing
and soaring high, way above best?
The days so warming, spirits fling
in the morning.

R. Tirrell Leonard Jr.

Across The Ample Sea

I stare across the ample sea
and wonder, of how time has passed
In you, I find a friend to be
I stare across the ample sea.

As dreams of sailing are recast
on tides and waves to ride alee
my loves a booming cannon blast.

So stirs my soul, betwixt and free
so smitten by your beauty's cast
I feel like falling through debris
I stare across the ample sea.

Love Once Knew

Love once knew the night stars
I dream you watch them too
and wish upon the avatars
love once knew.

The moon above once drew
my somber darker scars
to rest in fields of dew.

In the rising red Mars
I see the seas renew
on the tides and sand bars
love once knew.

The Last Farewell

1}

He waved good by as she left
the boy was sad as she went
he thought about the word goodbye
and wondered what was good.

2}

In the days since that farewell
he saw color drain from his eyes
things he touched, laid lifeless still
his world of fantasy had withered there
and still what good was goodbye
he left childhood there behind.

3}

In the summer he found solace in books
of Faulkner. Hemingway or Scott Fitzgerald
Hawthorne called out from the shelf
and the words of Lord Dunsany
each of fantasies dark and grand
led him to find H. P. Lovecraft
But where was good in goodbye, he soon forgot.

4}

Yet one day in August she had returned
and the color found his eyes had changed
dark and wondering still of dreams
"A Light In August," in his hands
He seemed older than he used to be
the boy had grown in her time away.
She wondered now
where's the good in goodbye?

Old Friends

1

Lightning cracks though the night with booming sounds
the kite comes down in flaming tatters all around us
as the thud of an old key hits the muddy ground
we are soaked through, hearing only the rain.

2

The smell of hot chocolate, our fingers warming on the mug
the marshmallows are melting into pools of white mist.
I watch the smile grow on your face as you take a sip
the warmth is melting the ice inside us, you were first always.

3

Ideas from childhood have come to me now, though it was you as we
did these things, which had the knowledge to do it right.
I was along for the ride, even when we rolled boulders
down onto garden gnomes to watch gravity at play.

4.

Though of Ben Franklin's experiment with the kite
we both got in trouble, though it was you who held the string
the lightning came for both of us, yet the old key glowing green
before it hit the ground all hot and steaming
we helped each other up, but it was always you then me.

In The Summer of 1985

In wisps of fog, remember castle grounds
I walked among the ruins on walls and sounds.

Two weeks we camped outside, in pouring rain
Irish boys played in mud, we ran and slid
In Portumna I wish I could remain.

Tallaght, we stayed a couple days and nights
A dance to haunt my life, my heart undid
I left a girl, my love behind, a kid
To dream of dancing with her then, delights.

A song to take away the dreams and pain
She came to me, I pushed away amid
I feel the loss, my faults in broken chain.

I walked among the ruins on walls and sounds
In wisps of fog, remember castle grounds.

Dreams In The Stars

As chaos screams on through my mind and soul
look at night to stars as wonders extoll.

As feelings grasp and holding still my thoughts
I listen where the sounds so know my name,
A game at first, seek and connect the dots.

To file away the salted wounds became
A way to pass the time, to dream in dreams
The stars above so tell the tales in streams,
Of fate reborn to live and laugh the same.

In shards of light I see the rare teapots
Remember teas and afternoons to frame,
Of campfires soaring through the night moonshots?

Look at night to stars as wonders extol
As chaos screams on through my mind and soul.

For Dianna

A girl from a town by the sea
Has me singing of friendship still,
Her shadow follows her with glee
A girl from a town by the sea,
As ghosts will wait she dreams so free
And time will sit down by her sill,
A girl from a town by the sea,
Has me singing of friendship still.
This light across a darker lee
A girl from a town by the sea,
The shoals will reel and shine for the.
As strength and faith in beauty thrill
A girl from a town by the sea,
Has me singing of friendship still.

R. Tirrell Leonard Jr.

The Highland Light

darkness drapes—cascading over
the famed highland light
eclipsed by thoughts
of this wanderer's delight
while estranged in the mists
by legends of yore and might

the sea roars (with an echo) in northern Truro
as the land falls before the sea
yet for beauty—and for imagery—
there is no-place I'd quite rather be

while held high in the thoughts of Thoreau
and the kinsmen of centuries to pass
it has proved an iron will—against the tides
to be an icon from the past
that shall surely stand before the last—

Authors Note

I'd like to thank my wife of nine years Nancy,
As well as Monique Gomez and Nelson Boyd
and the staff at Xlibris, without whom
This book would not be possible.
To my friends who if listed would fill
a book itself, and for Will Leura and Cuddy
for teaching me the joys of improv.
Thank you,

Robert

Edwards Brothers Malloy
Thorofare, NJ USA
December 4, 2012